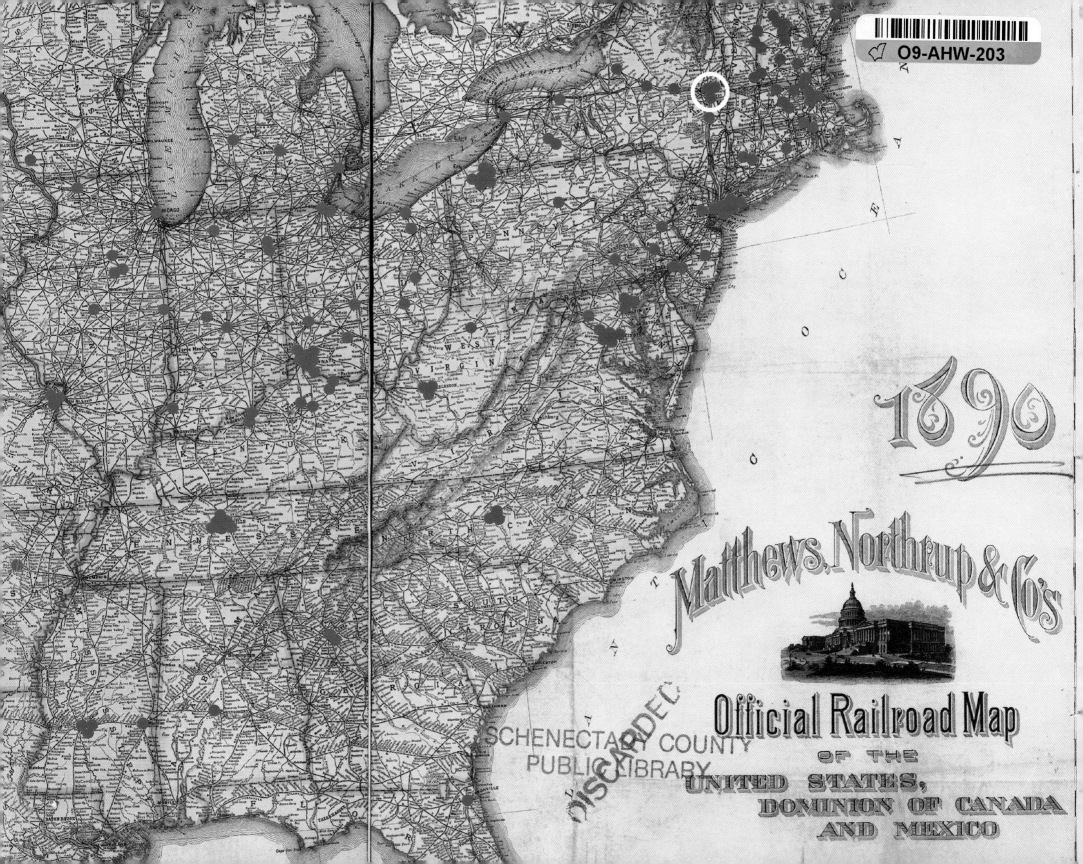

1890

Matthews, Northrup & Co's

Official Railroad Map

OF THE

UNITED STATES,

DOMINION OF CANADA

AND MEXICO

Nameless and homeless, the small dog shivered in the gloom. He was cold and soaking wet. The river was up, and in the darkness, he had fallen into the shallows. It was a bad night in Albany, New York.

Here was a lucky find, a space out of the weather.
The dog wondered about the piles of gray bags.
What could they be? Whatever they were, they smelled
good, and the room was warm.

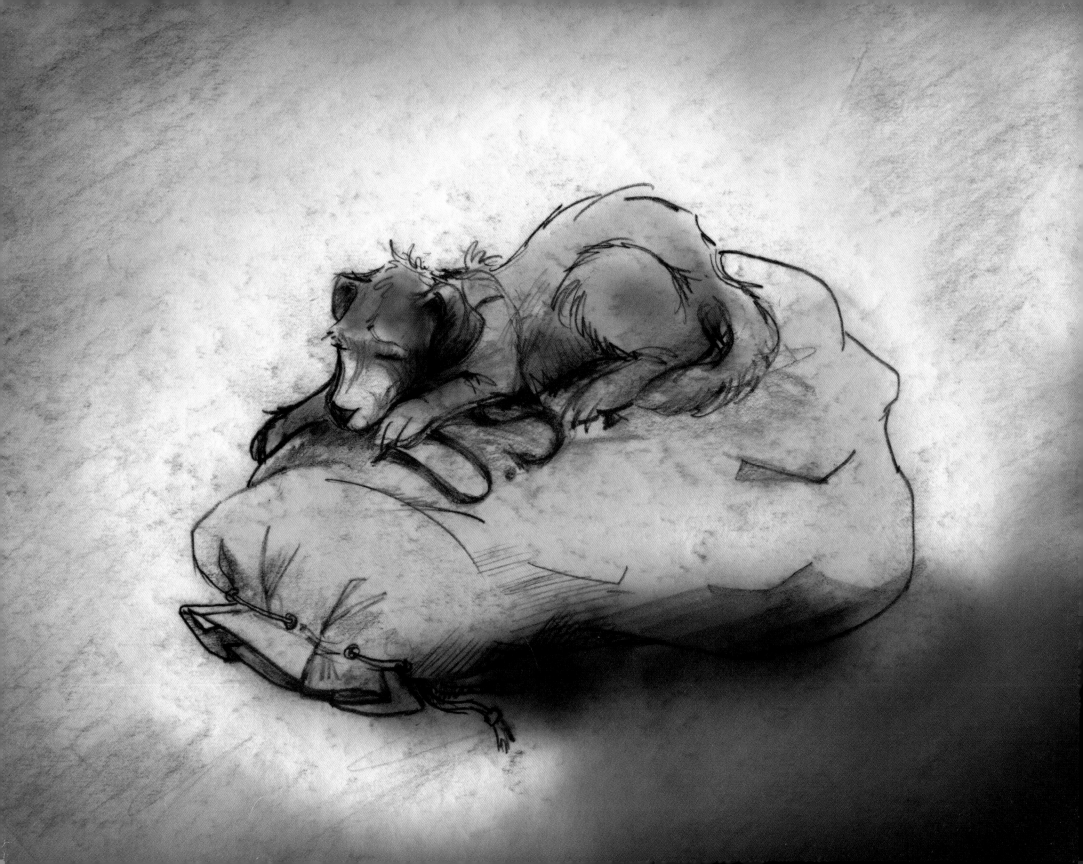

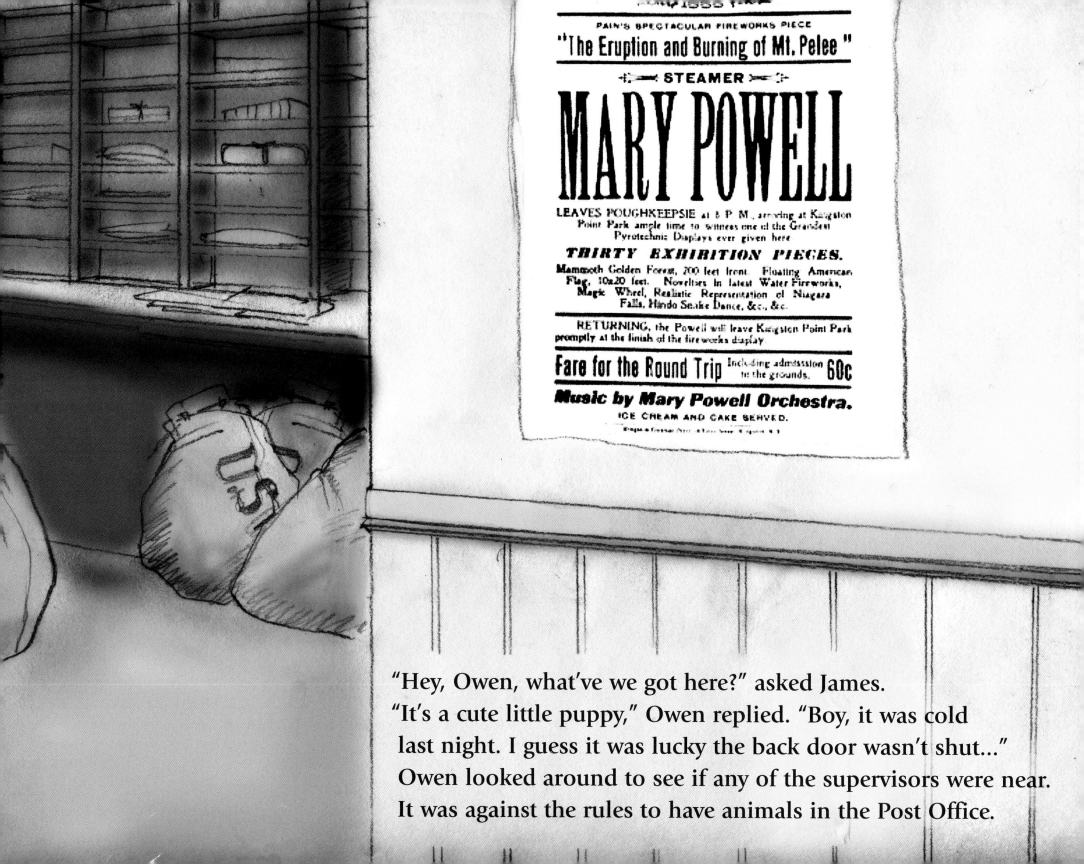

"Hey, Owen, what've we got here?" asked James.
"It's a cute little puppy," Owen replied. "Boy, it was cold
last night. I guess it was lucky the back door wasn't shut..."
Owen looked around to see if any of the supervisors were near.
It was against the rules to have animals in the Post Office.

The Supervisor heard about the dog the men were keeping. He came to investigate, asking why the dog was in the Post Office. James replied, "It's Owen's dog, sir. He's a cute one."

The Supervisor noted the pup's plaintive look, and in response, the dog wagged his tail.

"Won't do any harm to keep him, sir," said Owen. "He seems to love the mail bags, and just needs a place to stay..."

"... and some friends," said James.

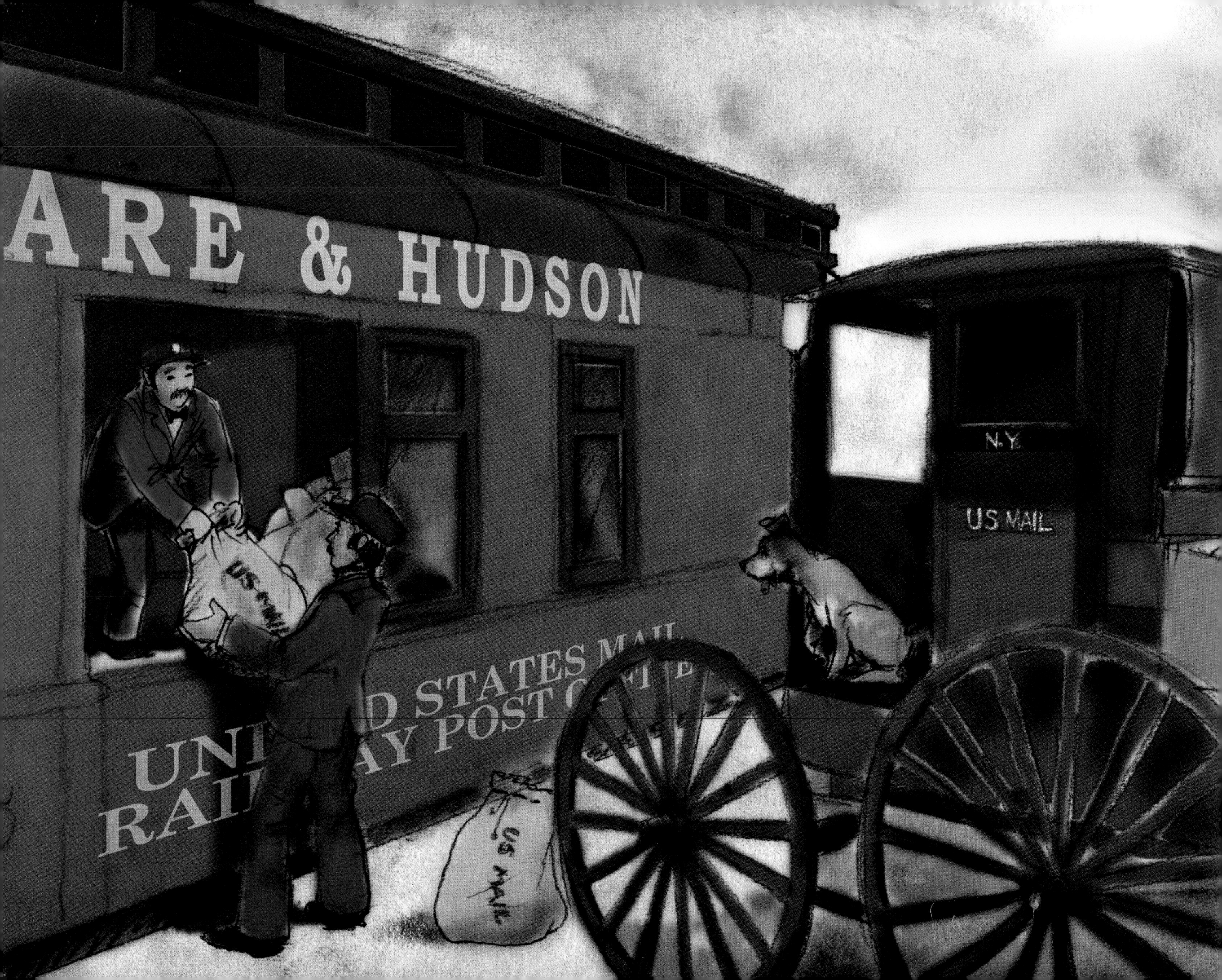
ARE & HUDSON
N.Y.
US MAIL
US MAIL
US MAIL
US MAIL

So time went on, and it got colder and then warmer, but the dog still had a home in the Post Office. He had a name now, too: Owney, for Owen's dog. He was allowed to go everywhere the postal workers went, and, one day, while watching them load a rail car with mailbags, he jumped in!

Wind whipped his ears. New smells filled his nose.
They were going so fast! Gosh, thought Owney,
this was much better than riding the mail wagons
all the time...142 miles to New York City and
142 miles back to Albany. That was a long way in 1889.
What a lucky dog!

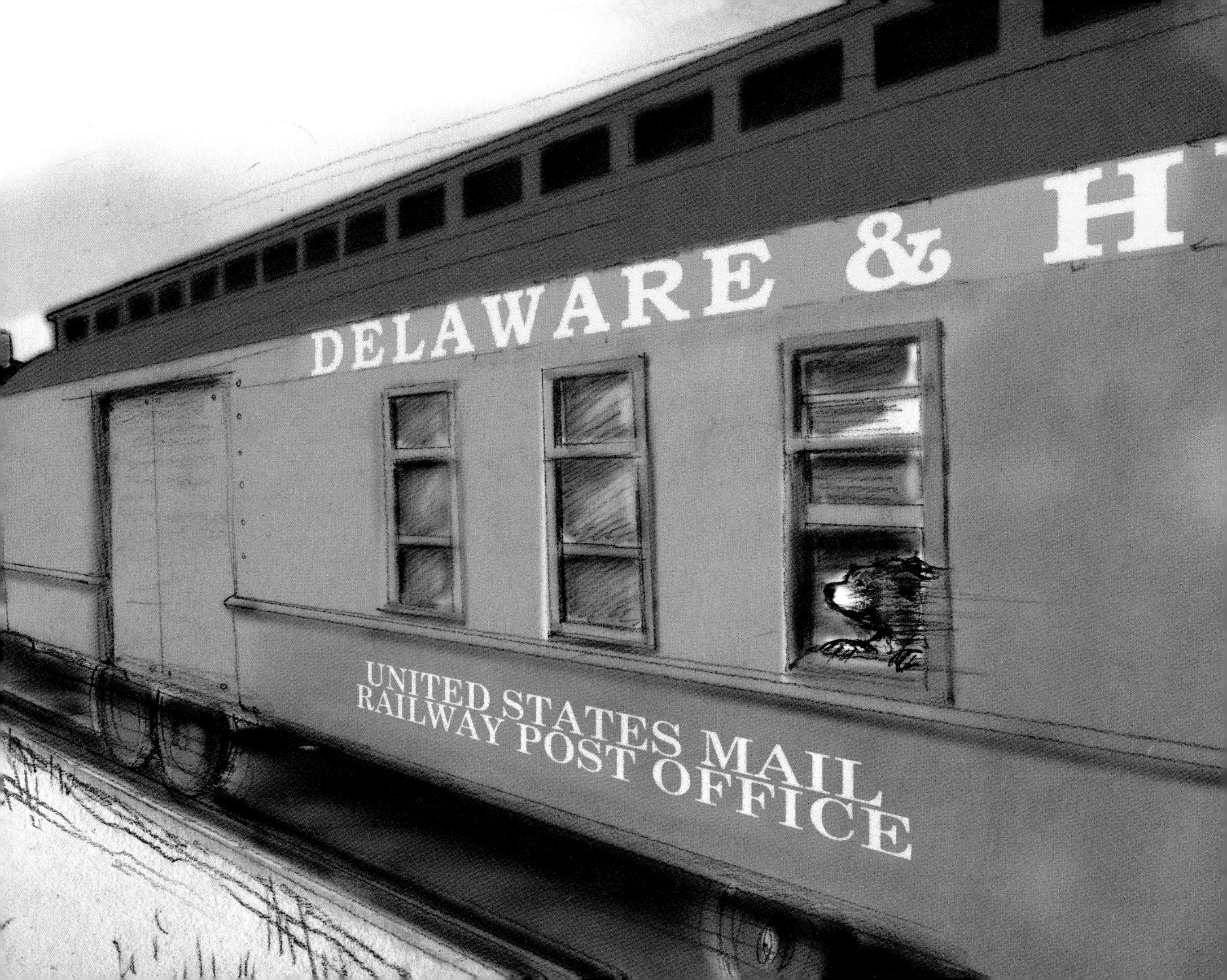
DELAWARE & H
UNITED STATES MAIL
RAILWAY POST OFFICE

Brookings, South Dakota

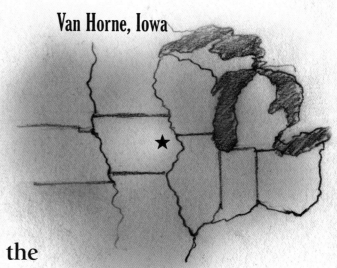

Van Horne, Iowa

"Say, how old are you, Owney?"asked Carl, the mail car supervisor. Because this is a true story, some of the questions are hard to answer; no one really knows.

Patting the dog, Horace said, "He don't know... just an orphan dog that crept into the Post Office one day and now gets to ride all the mail trains, eh, Owney?!"

"Lucky dog," said Carl.

Cloverdale, California

Paris, Kentucky

Owney had adventures at home, too. One day, everyone thought he was missing! The mail clerks unloading the mail expected Owney to be on the wagon because he was always so responsible and dependable; he was always where he was supposed to be! To make things worse, there was a missing mailbag, too... a double mystery!

Blocks away from the Post Office, Owney and the lost mail pouch were found. The pouch had fallen off the wagon and Owney had stayed behind. Someone had to protect the mail!

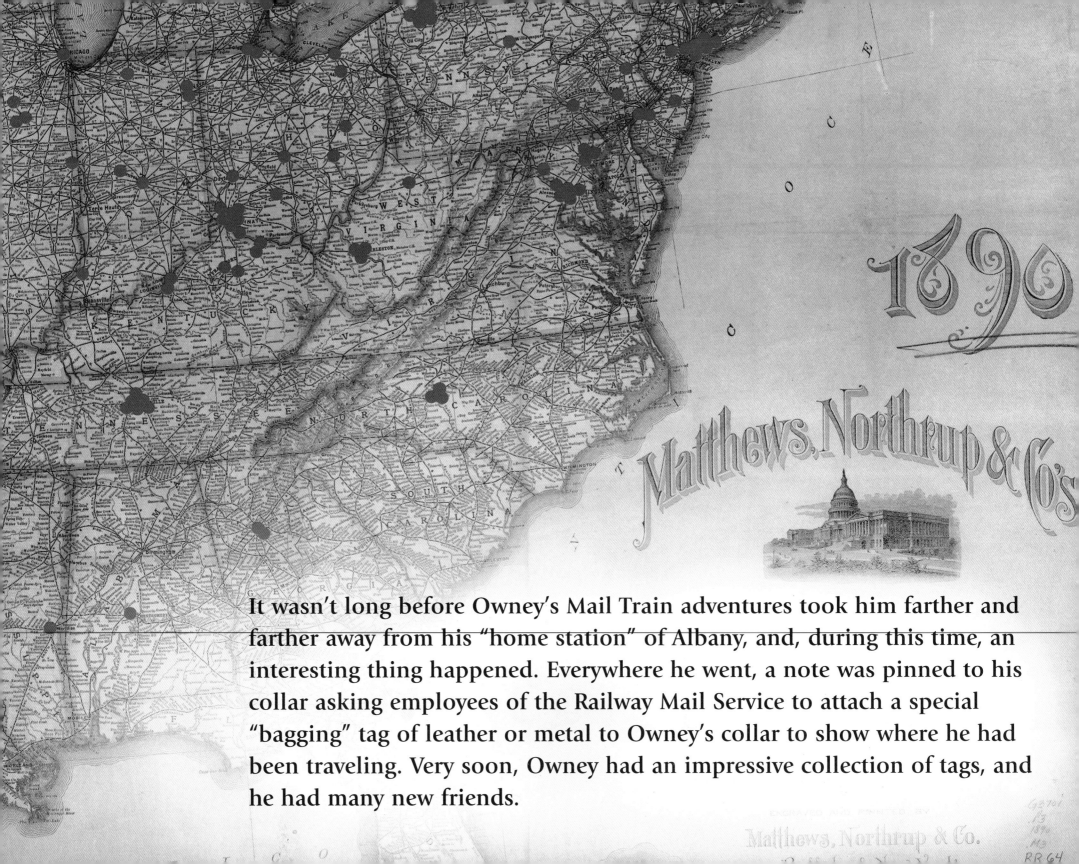

It wasn't long before Owney's Mail Train adventures took him farther and farther away from his "home station" of Albany, and, during this time, an interesting thing happened. Everywhere he went, a note was pinned to his collar asking employees of the Railway Mail Service to attach a special "bagging" tag of leather or metal to Owney's collar to show where he had been traveling. Very soon, Owney had an impressive collection of tags, and he had many new friends.

New friends like Winnona Kilbridge of the Los Angeles Kennel Club who gave him a medal for being the "Best Traveled Dog" of 1893, and Walter Banning of the Grand Rapids, Michigan, Dog Show who gave Owney a special medal.

Sissy Donahue, daughter of the President of the Pacific Kennel Club gave Owney an inscribed half-dollar and a special hug.

In Chicago, Mr. William Winter Wagner gave Owney a Globe Trotter medal. Little did Mr. W.W. Wagner know that this medal would represent a part of Owney's future!

Finally, Owney met the Postmaster General, John Wanamaker, who made a long speech about how Owney was now the Official Mascot of the Rail Mail Service. He presented Owney with a special jacket to carry his many awards and baggage tags.

Owney and his friends at the Albany Post Office learned that foreign travel could have its dangers. On a trip to Canada, Owney followed the mail bags into the Post Office in Montreal and was seized for not having a Canadian dog license!

When his friends in Albany learned of Owney's capture, they raised the $2.50 it would take to get Owney released and sent back to the United States. Close call, Owney!

Owney was famous now. He had traveled all over the United States, and many people were thinking he might be the first Postal Service dog to go around the world.

His friend Owen was worried. What if something happened to Owney in a far-away place and Owen couldn't get there to help him?

Still, one sunny morning in
August, Owney boarded a ship
and began the adventure of
his life.

...ended on December 29, 1895

Departed
August 19, 1895

...wearing his "bagging"
tag collection...

...and was greeted at home
by hundreds of admirers.

...with a tiny suitcase
containing a soft sleeping
blanket, comb and brush...

...gained six pounds...

132 days around the world...

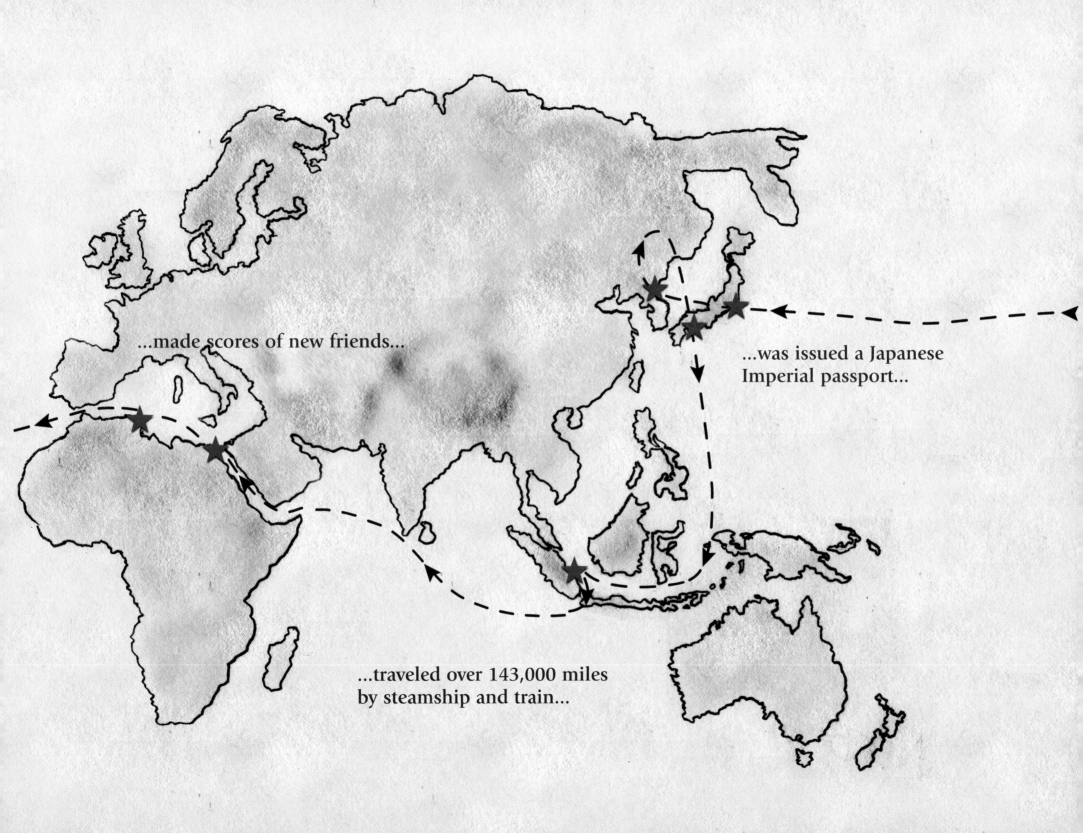

...made scores of new friends...

...was issued a Japanese Imperial passport...

...traveled over 143,000 miles by steamship and train...

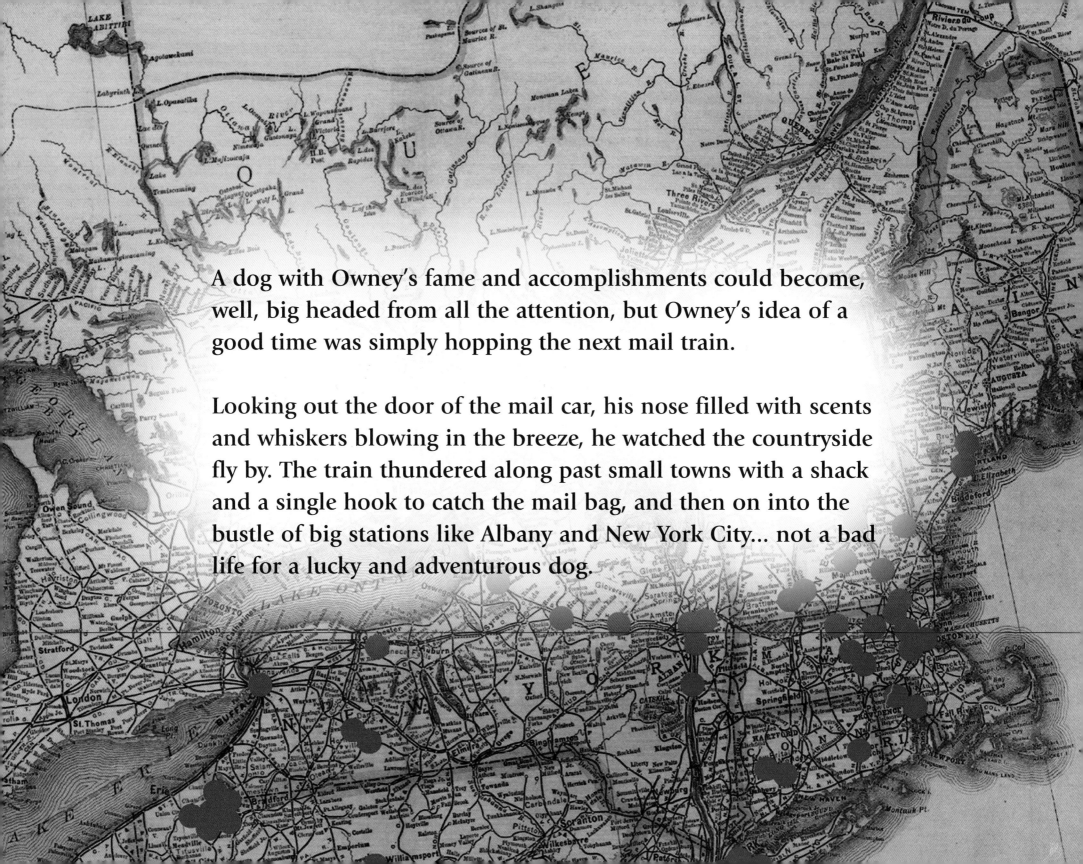

A dog with Owney's fame and accomplishments could become, well, big headed from all the attention, but Owney's idea of a good time was simply hopping the next mail train.

Looking out the door of the mail car, his nose filled with scents and whiskers blowing in the breeze, he watched the countryside fly by. The train thundered along past small towns with a shack and a single hook to catch the mail bag, and then on into the bustle of big stations like Albany and New York City... not a bad life for a lucky and adventurous dog.

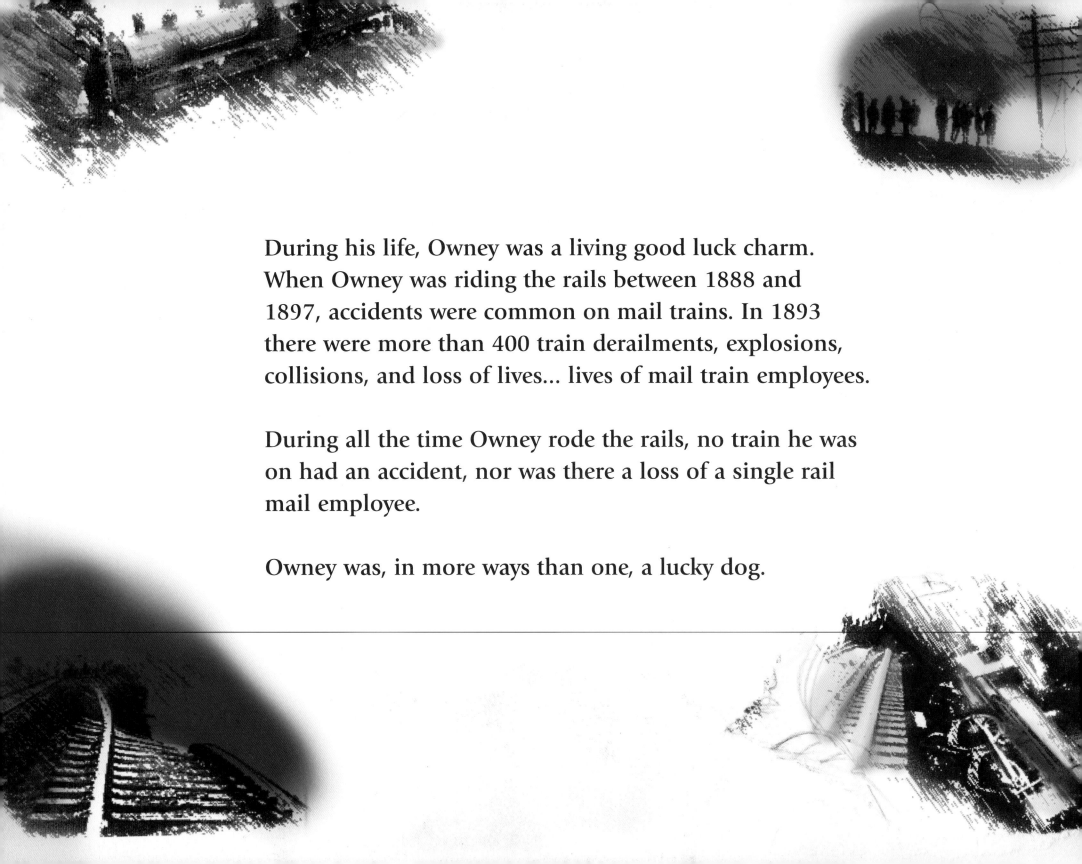

During his life, Owney was a living good luck charm. When Owney was riding the rails between 1888 and 1897, accidents were common on mail trains. In 1893 there were more than 400 train derailments, explosions, collisions, and loss of lives... lives of mail train employees.

During all the time Owney rode the rails, no train he was on had an accident, nor was there a loss of a single rail mail employee.

Owney was, in more ways than one, a lucky dog.

A Lucky Dog:
Owney, U.S. Railmail Service Mascot

Written by Dirk Wales
Illustrated by Diane Kenna

Our book is dedicated to stray dogs and warm places everywhere.

The authors wish to express their thanks for enormous assistance from:
Virginia Bowers, City Historian, Albany, New York
Megaera Ausman, Historian, U.S. Postal Service
Susan Novotny, Albany, New York
Jacket Design by C/Change, Chicago, Illinois
Lucy Morrison and Jeff Engel

GREAT PLAINS PRESS

ISBN# 0-9632459-0-2
Published by Great Plains Press
118 North Aberdeen Street
Chicago, Illinois 60607
fax 773-525-6278 or 312-850-0033

Printed in the U.S.A.

10 9 8 7 6 5 4 3 2 1